LESSONS FROM LINGERING HOUSES

SPECULATIVE POETRY
OF THE LAST UNDOCUMENTED WEATHER

KEN POYNER

Print ISBN: 9780578949901
Cover photo by Thomas Shellberg
Back photo by Matt Palmer
Author photo by Karen Poyner

Barking Moose Press

www.barkingmoosepress.com

Grateful acknowledgement is made to the following magazines, contests and institutions which first published many of the pieces in this volume, at times in slightly different form:

Alaska Quarterly Review
Altadena Review
Artful Dodge
Bad Henry Review
Blue Unicorn
Calliope
Colorado-North Review
Contact II
Cracks in the Ark
G. W. Review
Hiram Poetry Review
Indiana Review
Inlet
Iowa Review
Irene Leache Memorial Contest
Laurel Review
Litmag
Lodestar
Magazine of Speculative Poetry
New Mexico Humanities Review
Newsletter Inago
Ohio Journal
Old Red Kimono
Perspectives
Phoebe
Piedmont Literary Review
Poet Lore
Proof Rock
Pteranodon
Red Cedar Review
Sequoia

Sou'Wester
West Branch
Western Humanities Review
Wind
Windless Orchard
Yarrow

LESSONS FROM LINGERING HOUSES

Rooms

A MAN WHO HAS SURVIVED ON BARK

He could not let the wood go.
Deep in his stomach like pearl
It waited. Always as if by a back door
His wife prepared, burdening his plate with potatoes,
Chopping his meat into easily ordered pieces.
His food entered him as a man his last love.
Wine, cordials were nothing against his cellulose.
Slowly his wrists, growing stiff and unacceptable,
Began to thicken, his chest to barrel,
The edge of his toes to knot.
His fingers beat familiarity into the arm of his chair.
His wife would weep at lightning.
Mornings she would come upon him
Standing straight in the garden,
Naked toes searching the soil,
Rain on his upturned face,
Arms spread, fingers adequate for the sun.

He has collected a thousand axes
And made her hands to fit every one.

LEGACY:
McCLELLAN'S RUMORS OF THE BETTER LIFE

When the plow hit the first one I thought
Nothing of it. It happens. Occasionally
There is the skull of a horse, the skull
Of a man. The land is old; wealth
Accumulates. Splitting it, chalk dust
Spread on the underside of the soil,
I went on. The second was no different.
The bones in my field are my own:
I turn them over, spot the land with calcium.
Perhaps my plantings will grow bolder.
I could not break the fifth. Hard agate,
My plow blundered over it, left the ground
For twelve inches uncut. Small yellow mound
The skull jutted up and I worried the hard part
Would be an unusable tract, unprofitable soil.
Sixth, seventh, eighth, only one would break –
The other two solid, small markers, a threat
To more expensive machinery. Next, a skull,
A neck, a ribcage. A hammer will be needed.
At the end of the row a man's bones,
Complete, lie half out of the ground and
I must stop short. The damn things
Are now a litter everywhere. Maul tearing
Muscle from muscle I will need break the matter
To slivers, beat under the fragments. Wife,
The land is ours and still we must fight
To take out of it what we cannot use.
Here, roll these skulls into McClellan's garden;
The man has always loved a good story.
About these he should make a broad pass or two!

NOISE IN THE BATHROOM

I'm up all night while you're dreaming
Left to right. We've travelled a hundred
Thousand miles in open space, passed through
Uncountable laws of physics, pulled chemistry with us
Like a favorite plaything. The mere numbers
We've made all in one evening can cause a man worship.
This night you've breathed like a careless machine,
Turned over half a dozen times, smiled,
Snorted, brushed me twice with your leg.
I'm not responsible. The mean revolution speed
Of the earth doesn't change for a damn
And I come to hold the measurement in itself
Something. The rate of hydrogen depletion
Within a sun alters overnight – not measurably,
But a change. You sleep like a drunk bastard
Workman in the bed of a whore un-laid even
In the morning, half angered the money wasted,
Half glad the sleep. Cars work on the same basic
Principles twenty-four hours a day. The laws
Of Newton and Planck were the laws of
Isaac and Cain. You wake to think
I've been admiring your form in the sheets,
Waiting for you to stir so I can have you
First thing and if you're right one more time
I'll pack my bags, take up with someone my daughter's age.
You wake me like this, far too early, every morning of our vacation.

DROUGHT

One waits with all one's good urges
The rain, and its honorable occupation.
Chairs squeal on dry wood, the dust
Plays about in the yard. The sound
Of cicadas is less wet than usual.
Fence posts begin to flake. Through the house,
Open against heat, sun blows and beats
At the curtains – working into the closets,
The cracks between boards, until there is in the house
No dark place. Children have come to accept the land
As always cracked, the bushes as forever brown.
From the porch a man can watch for clouds –
Even with dust in the mouth, certain
Nothing can be done until the elements
Come rightly aligned – that planting in a dry field
Is wasted time. It is good to be the subject
Now and then of a much larger process.
One can wait with all one's good urges
And hope that yet another day the putting
Of things in their place goes on.

McCLELLAN'S LIST OF THINGS TO DO AT THE END OF THE WORLD

Clean the cats' bowls, or the roaches get in
And the cats eat the roaches.
Unplug all the electrical appliances.
Remove all the clothes from the back of the chair –
Placing the dirty ones that can still be worn
On the last of the hangers in the left of the closet.
Send the oldest son to the store for orange juice.
Suggest to the wife that the attic
Needs a good, all day, cleaning.
Your hands aching with the arch of trying them on,
Throw out the work gloves too worn or small to wear.
Give to the daughter the black stockings
The wife bought for after-hours
And has not worn since the grand embarrassment.
If it is before five in the evening
Bring in the morning's paper.
If there is to be company
Cancel.
Open the mail left for tomorrow
And answer the best of it.
Wave to that son-of-a-bitch next door.
If there is time to cut the ugly spot
Of grass on the front and side of the house,
Get at it hurriedly. If there is time,
Replace the one broken board in that
Damned ornamental fence. Shout back
At Henson's dog. Go to the barn,
Let out the cow that for years

Has given fair milk though
For the time, effort and cost
Milk is cheaper at the convenience store.
Clean out the straw, and shoot
The rats that have grown too large too easily.
Spread lime.
Walk the length of that cow's stall
As the cold animal stands in the yard it won't leave.
Use the rake to move the most of the stall's dross
To one corner. Check to see
That it is a damn sight cleaner
Than the cow would put up with.
Inspect shoes for manure.
Take a deep breath of the end of work.
Squat down. Wait.

TEACHING THE YOUNGER BROTHER TO DROWN

Quietly she slips out of her shoes
And rubs the base of her feet on wet grass.
This is it. She oozes out of her shirt,
Quivers out of her bra, places her thumbs
Inside the top of her pants and nods.
Dutifully I stumble out of my tennis shoes
And wrong-side out socks. I fumble with
My metal girder of a belt as she slithers
Out of her jeans, pulls her panties like a string
And waves them once above her head
Before hanging them in a tree. I am having difficulty
With my zipper. A quick leap and a bounce
And she is helping me with my shirt.
Things go faster than ever they did before.
The sun against my back is not as gentle
As she had told me it would be.
But even thus forewarned of her predictions,
Led at the end of her fingers, I follow her
Into the water. Oh, the water
Is no disappointment! Its green coolness
Flows between my knees and opens its mouth
Coyishly against my thigh. In the great surface
My hand does not disappear until
The wet is past my elbow. She kneels beside me
And her hair taps at my stomach
Without its usual cuts and slashes.
It is the lake's soft fur, not hers.
The ecstasy of mud between my toes, I begin
To run, leaping like a lead man against

The pliant coldness. My chest aches of water,
My teeth strain to clasp –
Her arms about my neck pull me to her quintessential breasts.
For no other reason, I cough.
The water at the tip of my tongue
Rolls like a shooter's marble.
Her red face rages frantically in a sea monster's grimace.
I swallow.

This will happen again.

LASTING ORDER

Mary Jo is singing again.
What she sings the last two weeks
The best of us have tried to divine.
Nothing common. Some who take their radios
Seriously have gone to new stations,
Put themselves around the dials and come up
With no clue. Old records are pulled out.
People who hum are asked from where the humming came.
No one minds that she sings. The curiosity
Of what she sings rubs us like an itch
Way down in new boots. The words
Are certainly of her own making, no sense,
And mouthed to suit her want; but the melody
Is more than something simply sung.
There is a time and fetching in it.
People tap it on chair arms and ask
Are you sure you haven't heard it?
Mary Jo sings and her song squats
Just outside the porch, scurries side to
Side for any listener – hard-backed
And maybe going soft only to shed on the full moon.
A man might pick it up at just the right time
And find a delicacy he can eat whole. But he can't
Be told what it is, and all to know about it
Is that it isn't unpleasant. And that she sings.

THE CAPITALIST

They charge you a nickel a throw –
When you're good and you keep
Coming back then it's a dime.
I take the baseball, wind up
Like a Palmer or Martinez, have
Too damn much arc on the ball,
Go over the man's head, a little
Anyway to the left. Someone behind me
Who is so damn good he shines of it
Gets two throws for a quarter, has
The quickest delivery I've ever seen.
The first ball scrapes just by the target's
Shoulder, and even at the regulation thirty yards
I can see him wince, shudder a bit
And try to draw himself smaller,
In upon himself and collapse like a bag.
The second pitch strikes him on the thigh,
Buckles him, almost sends him down on a knee –
But the man is good, recovers with the closed eyes
You come to identify with strength.
You should see it when they come up
With middling girls. A near miss and some
Go down. Things could get nasty
If they change the rules and bring the distance
Down to twenty-five yards, or all the way to twenty.
You've got some young farm boys can fling
Hell out of a ball, flat out kill a target on a one
Nickel shot, go to the end of the line
And burn another one for a dime. Sometimes

I think it would be better to go back
To hard work and necessary sleep,
Meals that keep the body from falling in
On itself. But we have our free time,
The wealth to turn into cash, an idleness
We bring down to the show tents, put into
A baseball: the thought of a target being struck,
The foam-like flesh, the bruises, the next ball
Rolled on the back of an expert's hand,
The excellent eye judging distance and wind.
This target rubs the thigh when he thinks
No one is looking. The two of us alone
With the projectile seller, I suspect the mark
Can be finished, sent for a few weeks
To the infirmary, and would like myself to see it.
I dig in my pockets hoping the feel of a quarter,
Counting the loose, glorious pennies.

GROUND ZERO

I cannot think that after all of it
The river will run any other way.
The bones of Jan McClellan will still
With the bottom mud be odd mineral.
In places the fence will yet stand;
Sections of porches, perhaps displaced, will sit
Off balance in fresh underbrush. Over everything
An anonymous Christ will still slowly reign.
Whatever you've left on the line will be gone.
In the metal box half a dozen papers
May persist: grandmother Rainer's picture,
Grandfather's World War I dog tags, the life insurance policy.
Facing east or north, if we sit on the stoop,
We may see the best of it. Our wedding picture
Wrapped in aluminum foil I've put in the old cartridge case,
That indestructible steel box spirited from the weapons range.
We can make certain in advance what will be left,
How the new races will know us.
Buried in the backyard is the family Bible,
Our full ancestry outlined in red. I do not think
Much of the topsoil will be removed,
That the hills will change. The county marker,
Our initials ragged on the side, will brood forever.
I can't believe that, in any real way, we will be gone.

If it comes in the south
We can watch from the kitchen window.

MECHANICS

Father comes down from the wagon, sets the reins
Over the seat back, and stretching as high as he can
Kicks the horse. I wince, but the animal could be stone,
Looks only ahead. I keep waiting
For the tail to flick, a hoof to lift
In the shifting of weight. The beast had been
The last hour slowing down, center of the road
And undistracted, but coming to little more
Than a shuffle, and then a stop. The cart
Loaded with information creaks, and my father
Would give his arm for three wheelbarrows.
Mother and I get down, at the wagon's rear
Stuff in our pockets as much as we can,
Fold fact into the spaces between shirt and skin.
We hold our arms out and father fills their
Bowl roundness, scoops information into his own
Cupped limbs, balances the overload against his chest.
I think I will never walk so far, will spill
What seems likes tons of obscurities: knowledge
Bouncing across the packed-earth road, being lost
In the ditches. Father plans to take another horse,
Come back later – hopes the local peasantry will not
Too greatly steal from the remaining stack,
Perhaps drawing off only handfuls of understanding at a time.

Back at the wagon, a sturdier horse in tow,
He finds the locals thick as cloth,
The obdurate horse down and drawn to ribs, even
The entrails going away in buckets, good meat
The object of quarrels. The pile of information

On the wagon is, if anything, even larger, fatted
With added fact, and he returns to us
With only the horse he took. A week,
And we tell him we are sick of horsemeat:
But we eat flank and heart and hoof-gristle
And he is happy a little while longer.

REINFORCEMENT

I am holding onto the rope.
This thing is a cheat: a man
Just can't bring himself to do it.
Swaying back and forth, arm tense,
The world looks still the world.
I should have tied my hands,
Made the drop a much farther one.
Any fellow who ties the rope to a low tree limb,
Stands placidly in a chair,
And jumps off,
Is destined to failure. The land
Spins and turns before the body;
The greenery, the thought of growth,
Surrounds the man and his act.
I am holding onto the rope.
I have thwarted myself again.
Letting go of the cord would be
No change of perspective – only
Being tied, unable to intercede,
Could change the point and drive.
Suspended here, in charge of himself,
The man is still the man,
The man still sees with eyes
The man harbors day to day.
I am holding onto the rope.
Flat footed on the ground, the chair
Knocked away behind me, I want
A knife to cut this umbilicus
Or the mob to fasten it higher in the tree.

Bind my hands. Let my feet kick for air.
I am holding onto the rope.
The hemp wraps loosely about my fingers.
Let one other take hold of it.

EVENT HORIZON

The deer's head on the wall, the antlers
Mounted, I wanted to know where
The face went. Father pointed out
The eyes, the nose, the teeth. Above
The television set, as much fur
As the rug, the head sits goliath. Venison
For three weeks has been better
Than hamburger, chicken, fish. Standing
In a chair I can rub the flat
Of the forehead, the close hair.
Father explains how for hours he waited
Still in the woods, rifle close to his chest
For cold. The animal burst at full speed
From brush straight at the man and
He pulled the trigger, tracked blood,
Pulled the trigger again. The hide was no good.
We have meat and trophy. The cost
To mount the thing is mother's thought
Of her new coat and Jamie's shoes.
Since the head has come to us
There has been no face on the TV set.
Even the dog next door has come
To utility packaging: Mrs. Meyers down the road
Has ceased to look unalike. I am
Beginning to wonder who in the glass at morning
Is looking back to me. I think
Of my mouth as orifice; I talk to Father
With noise. From our plaque on the wall
The deer watches: milk sight, Punic stare.
I want to know what a radio telescope sees.

POLITICAL SYSTEM

They're hanging the men two to a limb
And I am afraid already one limb
Has broken and a knee in both backs the nooses
Had to be hand tightened. There was no time
To put the women away and they saw
How close we have sometimes to come to method.
There are none among us experts; we get
A bit sloppy and the children see that as well.
A group of men clearing out the north end
Have taken to dragging back their catch
And fewer are left in any shape for the trees –
And so less demand. When we run out of rope
We'll fashion bedsheets together. All across the fields
The wives and children are wandering,
Quiet for the most part and glad to be left alone,
Yet with a few howls and pointing fingers. I wish I had not
Laid in seed on my last track, for there is
No way of keeping them out. At the house
The wife took in the Thompson family,
And her good graces important, I'll end up
Raising Jim Thompson's two girls, though the bastard
I just strung up an hour ago. Four years
The price of wheat has been dropping, the payments
On machinery falling behind, the children
Doing without. They'll not play us one
Against the other again, call us out
To cut our own throats and take a price
Too low to plant for next season. The Simpson boy
Inherits his father's land and you'd better

Put him up alongside. Twice as much land
Per man and the will to organize. One more year
And I'll thumb the pages of the Penney's catalogue clean.

NOAH (II)

We sweep mud out of the living room.
A lion walks by the front door,
Looking hungrily in and the peaceable beasts
Had better increase their numbers
First act on land, or we will lose
Species after species. You opened both ends of the Ark,
Cried joyously as they stumbled wobbly-legged off,
Fell to their sides with unsteadiness.
We will all make a life of seaweed
Until spring, the salt dries out
And the grasses begin again. I have
Two rooms swept out, though
We will never get the mud out of the cracks.
The closet shelves are full of dry fish,
Caught when the waters went down.
Everything of value has floated away. The chairs,
The bed, are God-knows still drifting in some ocean
Or deposited half-way around this new world.
Heathen bodies most likely still cling
To anything that stayed above water:
Dead fingers I'll not pry from any object
To make it mine again. You shove mud
And muck and seaweed and sea-logged wood
Out of the door and off the porch steps;
I watch you shimmer in what little light
Reflects down to these depths. An elephant
Works lugubriously by, a step at a time,
And it is your strength that has kept us
From the disaster so long, saved us time and again,

Made us believe. Husband, captain,
You and I are the fishes.
Your gills flare below your ears with effort
And what floats on the surface far above
Neither of us can see. Our first dinner
Off the barge I've cooked without fire
And gathering for it already we are troubled
To keep our feet on the floor, walk with legs,
To not adore the smooth esses of the oxen
Passing gracefully the second story window. Consciously
Heel to toe, I love your foolish bravery,
But it is time to be practical.

PRIVATE PROPERTY

Bent over the hoe she stands
Keeping time in the garden,
Ragged dress drawn up about her knees,
Hair hidden beneath a scarf.
The young plants hesitant on mounds
Shudder for the near miss of her instrument.

By the bonfire in the common field
Couples dance idiot dances with no steps,
Frolic like bears, twisting immodestly
In their best peasants' clothes. Bread flourishes:
Corn, salads of diverse kind, kingdoms
Of wild meat, the landlord's gift pig.

His bride continues,
Dragging the errant grass from the shade
Of tomato, corn, bean, salad fodder,
Making dust the surface of her land.
Sweat darkens her gown like the water of drowning.

Scarecrow, he stands cataract, waiting.
The productivity of the dance
Stolen from his feet –
The male momentarily counterbalanced by his female:
The two of them,
As in the first night of a second marriage,
Grateful.

CHRISTMAS

The ash in the fireplace stirs
And on my feet I draw
My cudgel to the ready, set my legs
To the act. It is only the last
Of a forgotten ember and I back
Cautiously to the chair, lay my instrument
Against the arm rest, lose my weight
To plundered furniture. The tree blinks.
Across the mantle four stockings
Hang empty and rotten: my sons', my wife's,
My own. I am not one to let indignity lie.
On the end table milk and cookies,
Ordered meticulously and left in blind anticipation
By my children, await the man about whom
The season revolves. I am warm
In a cold house; my wife asleep
Turns over in her tattered nightgown; my sons
Go to bed in aged underwear and socks.
With excitement the boys stare
At the cracks in the paint of the ceiling.
Worst of all, in the morning – slumped
Like a carnival bear, sleeping, my axe handle
Fallen to the floor – packages,
Bright paper will spread around me
And I will think first of all
What those marked with my name might hold.

CHRISTMAS BY THE LAKE

Night creeps over the ice like a hunter.
The metal of its spear gleams from my porch roof.
Come into the house; I must latch the door.
The lake rises from its tomb and dances
In the moon's frigid sigh. Wolves
Chuckle under the eaves. Dogs
Fat with snow circle the wood pile
Waiting for the fire to sputter.
Owls in the dark can take your eyes
For starving mice. Never mind the bones,
Those long white fingers still at the window sash.
They belong to no one you know.

CURRITUCK, N.C.

I expected it of the children.
And McClellan. I always knew
He was at the edge of something,
Clinging on at best, somehow
Not able to keep up. I knew
As well they'd use night for cover,
Use the open land near my stretch of the woods.
I expected the murdered stock,
The fires, the howlings of ritual group sex,
The jousting matches, the rapes, the selling
Of slaves, the tearing down of my fences, the accidental
Fouling of my machinery. I saw it coming.
I've been telling you for years.
During the day we see only a few:
A small amen corner copulating on a roof,
A boy racing by in a boar's head,
Two girls arguing over a bearskin.
I work around the house, stay away
From the outbuildings, the forest edge.
I always kept a good stock of ammunition,
The rifle clean, put up new, strong shutters,
Extra locks on the door, laid in
Good canned stocks. By the time the countryside
Was filled with naked dentists and doctors,
Clerks from the package store, we had ourselves
Set to last as long as it took. Thank God
The scent was in the air months ago,
I went about collecting the feathers. I gathered
Dozens from the ground, pulled pounds of them

From the birds I caught in snares,
Stored them in grocery bags. The place
Was getting thick with them; I began
To worry the decline would not come about.
Once we've got them knitted together, put ourselves as tightly
Into them as into our common skins,
The rabble will come to our front yard
And believe us on the roof practically Gods,
Chieftains, prove that order and forethought
Are as much a key in the primitive as in the complex.
Hold to civilization a little longer and we
Shall have the best, the fattest, of the roasted boys.
Keep dancing naked on the porch, and I'll cut you out of everything.

STATE RELIGION

Myrna on her front porch is speaking in tongues.
This is not the demonstration that in the revival tent
You clap for, dance in your place for,
Believe, and maybe fall yourself
Into possibly holy languages. Not
The demonstration that, as one who did not go,
You laugh about, and wonder
How much the whole affair to the minister
Brought in. It is ten o'clock in the morning.
Good people stand in her front yard.
Gardens are left half weeded. One
Riding lawn mower is still running in idle.
A basket of clothes sits on the ground
By a clothesline leaning to the side
That already has clothes hung on it.
Dogs get out by fence gates left open.
Men stand in the yard with hoes
And grass shears, in shirts they never wear
Outside of their own fences,
Their hands reddened with oil or grass stains
Or the imprints of wrenches. Women
Leave their hands in the pockets of housecoats,
Or hold loosely children, looking
Beyond Myrna and her house, out into the Sound
Where this morning boys are looking to empty
Other people's crab-pots. A storm will be up
This afternoon and the boys are never watching.
Myrna's yard then will be half mud.
Who would dare not to come.

Her words sneak along the porch, fall
Down the steps, collapse on the ground between listeners.
The bright red edges of her day dress
Slip away from the breeze and hang at attention.
When will this be over.
To shift a leg is impolite; to go home
Dangerous. Even older children fidget and look back
To houses that are forgetting their occupants.
A car passes on the state road, above the speed limit,
The driver not even turning to look.
Myrna is known to be long winded.

INDIAN MASSACRE

The cavalry is coming over the hill.
Horses pound mordantly at stone;
Men dressed in dapper blue draw swords,
Dinged service revolvers. Wild
To keep his wind and his horse
Under control, the bugler lifts his head
Unto God and sounds of urgency.
Rescuing legions of men
Upright in their saddles prepare
To be the need and agent of thousands
Of shopkeepers, farmers, homesteaders,
Cattlemen, children, bankers,
Prospectors, women hanging clothes and
Worried the passion of the savages in this land,
Rail layers, builders of towns and mines,
Traders, trappers, the flowers that transplanted
Grow in the desert. Raging, clattering
Out of the dim horizon the company of men
Melts into a dot of blue correctness.
Worried the clear morning may fail
To an afternoon of cooler rain, a woman
Makes her fire of small sticks, stirring ash.
Inside the skin tent her man, fresh
From the violence of lovemaking,
Stretches into his cloak, rolls the bedding
Belonging to his wife and children into a neatness.
Today there is more wood to be gathered,
A rabbit to chase too far, a readiness
In the pit of his eldest son's stomach to be filled.

A man in his time may have many things,
Passing them to his children imperfectly,
The rough of charred wood.
A child, unafraid of anything the land
Might cause to exist against him,
Knows the morning meal will be yet
A while and wanders far from camp.
He will be the first.

THE AMNESIAC'S WIFE

A stone
At the bottom of a casual river,
Lying with ten thousand stones,
Content to feel water run over me.

This woman is not so pretty.
She could never, like the quartz pebbles
Children flick privately into the water,
Gleam and postpone herself.
She is too sure of her point of reference,
Too willing to be a map of wide locations.

Once, though, I'm told
I lay upon her like quartz
Resting on the mud floor of the river's house.
Her long hair
Has wrapped around me like sediment
And we together have made the sound of running water.

She is not so pretty though
As the sight of plankton galaxies drifting past.
And she, unlike the water,
Urges too much.

THE BRUTE

You've brought in the wood,
Placed a clean carcass in the oven.
The husband has been gone an hour, will be gone
Maybe two more, at least one and a half.
The two children are tagging behind him
In supply and specialty shops, squealing voices
Like the rusty door of a wood stove.
Everyone is wrapped deep in cloth while you
Drag your bare feet over the carpet, gaze
Out of the sweating window at the snow field
Unmoved this hour. One hawk
Drifted above the white blindness,
Twisted over your chimney and headed
Into town. His wings
Taught you conservation of motion
As you wrapped yourself naked in the curtains,
A predator. The back door is open;
You race out, rolling in the snow by the porch
Like the white wolf, rubbing the color
Into your fur, becoming a coldness
Invisible to all but the most frightened eye.
The woods have forgotten you.
You wait, crouched on your hind legs,
Nose held into crystal air for the target scent.

Before you go home to bathe
You will feel the fear of a rabbit in your mouth –
But already you can hear the lynching sound
Of your husband starting back from town:
The immaculately killed meat bounding in the Chevrolet's trunk,
A lace negligee for you sly on the front seat.

LOVING THE CIRCUS

They put the whole damn thing up
In two days, tore hell
Out of McClellan's south field.
They took down a full strip of fence
And I bet, though they have pledged
To put it up again, it will stay down.
I'd never let it go on on my land.
I'm sure the cut is good – but all
The trash, the styrofoam and plastic,
The ruts. Then again, McClellan,
His wife and skinny children, each night
Turn out their lights and think
Of the elephants, the lions, zebras,
Monkeys, dogs and showgirls just across the yard
Bedding down or rehearsing. He has the right
To stand around as the tents go up,
To ask pertinent questions, to not be
An intruder. We plan to go
The last night of the play, slip twice
Through the sideshows, the Big Top once.
Our children will lie seriously planning
In their beds to run off and be clowns, to learn
To order the large cats, to swing
In air like late summer's lightning.
McClellan's boys after supper lean
On their manure shovels, spread the issue
Over their mother's garden. The man
Will be sure to get everything he can,
And the boys will be glad when the
Sequined, balsawood crowd is gone.
They wanted my land. I thought better.

RESPONSIBILITY

The water is not deep enough to hold him forever.
Most likely the crabs will find him in the reeds,
Fishermen from Norfolk trip over the bones a year later.
Cut down the marsh, dredge the end of your dock,
Make a bulkhead, and it's what you get.
A bit of moss, cattails, the water
For several yards hardly more than a foot deep,
And the boy would have to have been
Damn stubborn to make himself drowned.
His parents walk the limit of their backyard,
Flashlights and the foolishness to call for the lost child.
They look off the end of their land
As though the water would not take a new gift
An inch out of the way, as though
The Sound did not hide its useful collectibles.
I've filled out my own backyard, strung
A bulkhead, dredged the boat slip
To a full six feet. Summers you can take the lawnmower
All the way to water, run one wheel
On the board atop the buttress, escape having to trim
Altogether. But I have no children.

THE FARMER'S DAUGHTER,
THE TRAVELING SALESMAN

On the front stoop two days
You've been camping with your sack of wares.
Glass flowers, electric candles, mechanical
Powder sets, musical whatnot boxes. Yesterday
You held to the living room window a satin nightrobe;
Day before it was Indian feathers, rhinestones.
I'll not pull my hands out of the melon rinds
To answer your knock. Burlap bag and suitcase,
You can sit at my door and hope,
But with the indoor plumbing I will
Outlast you. If you think I'll let you in
For the cold, you've gone wrong again.
Last night as you slept, curled dog
At the base of the steps, I slipped
A half pound of beef, two rolls and coffee
Through the torn screen and you should
Take the strength to walk. Stereopticon.
Blue garters. Lint brush. All the curtains
Are drawn, blanket strung across
The thin ones. You wave your hat,
Crank in the front yard a jack-in-the-box.
All this morning I kept to the bedroom,
The sheet pulled around me. You're damn good,
You son-of-a-bitch. When I come out,
My best and a broom, you have better
Be single, have the Dr. Shung's Magic Copper.

THE LAST GRACEFUL HISTORY

I go out with our youngest boy in tow
And you say nothing. He's been
At the cat's tail again, trying
By strength of arm to lengthen it.
Last time it was an attempt by him
To prove a gymnast from the kitchen table.
A trip out to the barn for a little bit
Of the negative end of Skinnerian psychology
Is the thing I can remember my grandfather
Telling me about almost with nostalgia.
His father at other times never seemed so large.
Always it was to hurt the striker
More than the one who was struck:
And even when the boy being struck
Became the man striking, he didn't believe it.
Two generations, and we go back:
Pick up the old practices, regard ourselves
As rustically pragmatic. The boy yells a bit,
In an hour once again is acceptable to the family,
Is let off without the stigma you find
Brooding in the modern punishments. It was
Your idea. Often I'll come in to find you
In the pantry with sapling in hand, the boy
Already sent for the ruin of a barn that years ago
May have served some useful purpose.
My right arm is learning the motion.
The thing in itself separates us from most the near families,
And for it I think I am dressing more conservatively.
The boy today is surer of consequences than ever in his life again he will be.

An argument over something, words
That a century earlier would have a woman,
Let alone a girl, burnt – and our daughter
Of thirteen smashes a glass against the sink.
You go for a broom and I go for her wrist and
I'm headed out to the barn face up
Like a man with an inheritance to spend
And you stop me less than halfway.

Only after the fact, after catching my breath
For all of an hour as though with a net,
Can I understand why you are the best you have ever been,
The best I could ever want. Sapling at bedside,
We've gone too far for this to work.

WAR FEVER AND THE FIRST STRIKE

Myrna's got the gossip again.
My wife and she lean across the fence,
Two left arms on the metal top pole.
I put that fence up only to keep the dogs
Close to the house and this weekend
Sometime I'm going to have to fill in
The holes they've dug under it.
The clothes will be dry by the time
The women are finished ascribing their wants
To neighbors and travelling salesmen.

Out in the Sound, a wader fisherman
Is working along the edges of my boat slip
And I'd like to tell him about that huge
Water moccasin that last week I tried
To use my 22 to pop the head off of.
I could hear the shot whistle from its ricochet
Through the woods, watched the snake
Undisturbed swim somewhere in, just about
Opposite where the wader fisherman now stands.

He flings the lure in high arc, begins reeling
Long before the plug hits water.
Later this afternoon I might get up
To standing on the bank, making a few
Casts. Weather holding out, we'll set up the grill,

Do in a few steaks this afternoon. Saturday,
And the kids already on the road,
Too damn fast, dressed too damn sloppily
Or scantily. The wife shifts, Myrna

Raises a finger in affirmation. The McPhearson boy
Goes by in his third-hand car, clipping
Both shoulders of the road and I can imagine
What he would be in the city. The fisherman
Walks on, dragging his inner-tube, pulling
From a pouch a beer. I feel sinfully a little
Relieved he is going to fish along someone else's bank.

A sure stop to gossip, I step out to the fence,
Smile, ask of Myrna's husband. Any time
Our children, and hers, will be back from
Moyock Amusements, broke, a little expectant
Of more, a little angry that not much
Goes on thirty miles outside of the city. But
It is at least an hour or so before – too many
To a front seat – they skid across the gravel driveway.
And of that time I want to get the best use.

BACKWATERS

There have been fewer people about.
Each week the number of children
Tearing down my fences has gotten less.
I've not chased a mating couple out from the grove
In six months and I just about
Miss the sport. Cars going by
Have halved. Fishermen, climbing into the canals
All across the back of McClellan's land,
Have dried up to practically nothing.
A new by-pass, and the county loses twenty years.
Our crop is less molested, but I plant it
Only for the subsidy. We have fewer
Young families with Pennsylvania license plates
Stop and ask after the highway junction. Admitted –
We were always simply on the road between
Two places. Yet, I'll miss the added traffic,
The Simpson girls turning on all the lights in their bedroom
And stripping down to slips. Two more years
And they'd have been to pure skin.
Still, the cars would have gone past –
No loss of speed, an occasional horn,
Some hooligans stopping to drink in my soy.
We'd not have slowed them with metal barricades;
But the girls would have thought nonetheless
They were contributing, making something of themselves,
More than toy farm utensils. You could have brought me
Tea on the porch as I watched them, raised hell
At me and glanced at their window yourself – feeling
With the traffic, equal to two fleshed skeletons.

You know I'll soon take up again my midnight walks.

COMING OF AGE

We wait with the covers pulled to our chins,
Lie flat on our backs, know it is morning
And know it is too early. Mother and Father
Stumble about, rattle the objects on their dresser,
Make the sounds of quieting one another
And are certain we are awake. An hour,
And the five of us are in the street, wrapped
To the shape of eggs – I am the warmest,
The youngest with the greatest number of larger things
That will fit. Father, worried by the crowds,
Stuffs from his pocket into my inner-most coat
His gray purse, buttons all my garments
To my neck, lets me walk beside him with a hand
All to myself. Out from between houses
Neighbors come like pets on a raining day,
Fill in the open space before and behind us,
Settle easily into our pace. Sitting on his
Wagon platform, at town center, the iconographer
Watches a time-piece for his hour of opening,
Does his figures. I've never seen so much mud
In one flat place and more than all the neighbors
Fill the square around his wagon, wait
The one day for selling. Something happens.
The man stands up, goes beyond the blankets
Separating the back of the wagon from the platform
And Father lets go of my hand, reaches
Into my clothes for the lumped, sweating purse.
<>

On the way home, my father carries a box
In both of his hands. Mother and I
Run ahead, look behind the trees and in the ditches
At each intersection, hold each other's hand as though
To escape a gas. Mother shakes, pulls me
To the folds in her rotting dress, to Father
Way back on the wet road shouts
Hurry, it's almost dark!

CHILDLESS WOMAN

You have the lids on tight,
The seals pieced into place.
In the back room, as well arranged as a church,
They await the laying on of hands,
The signal that it is they who are now in season.
The yellow curtain to the pantry is kept open a crack
So you may watch them in their vestibule.
Sun reflected from the kitchen gathers on their cold glass.

A whorehouse of jars, the shelves strain.
Your husband has put up another support,
Told you the next garden must be less.

You are counting the days until
The first jar of corn will be opened.
Yesterday, you found the tomatoes
Crossed over, in the lap of the peas.
Though once a week you move them to the front
The beans have been fond of the far corners.

You have the lids on tight,
But capture your breath before entering the pantry.
A bit of zucchini has made it to the floor
And is vainly rolling after your feet.
You place it back on the shelf. Next year
The garden will be two more yards in breadth,
Another five in length. The spike of your hoe
Will be the strength that is growth,
The horror that is harvest.

SOCIAL BLOCK

Grandmother looks from her window:
Her thin frame the device the family
Has come to be based upon. She makes
No decision, but the honor is hers. Dust
Rises waist high and in the heat
Grows to mud against our legs. Judith
Has the better of it. Taller
Than her sister she has the longer reach,
The more powerful swing. Susan
Dodges and hopes to find the opening,
To slip in under the blows and find
The one killing punch. Their father on the porch
Is proud the stamina both his girls show.
Dark hair flies in ringlets. The mother
About her pair like a moth pokes
And separates, keeping the girls' anger
At the level of skill, enforcing the fair match.
My girl has no sister and will when the time comes
Take the loser here. My three sons,
Aware the flesh to be graded today,
Sit on the fence rail and remark
The quickness of leg, the firmness of arm.
Good backs; strong breasts; hard, leather thighs.
Wives have their demand and purpose. I would
Were it not for age consider the winner of this.
In the field cattle are tired of waiting.
The victor's feast is solid and mechanical:
It is time for the knife,
It is time for the meat to have its place.
I throw a stone at the pair and
By hundreds the fury grows.

THE LAST BELIEVER AT ARMAGEDDON

The most of us are not taking sides.
We have enough to do to stay out of the way,
To avoid the occasional misfires, to sidestep
Whatever angel or demon happens to hold
The greatest sway in our neck of the woods.
Whole towns are leveled. City blocks
Boil to colored glass. Houses
Just by the passage overhead of thunderbolts
Or blue flame shiver themselves to splinters,
Fall in, and we no longer bother
Trying to pull survivors out. One angel
Lit on our roof, and knowing what fire
It would draw, we raced out near to naked –
Headed straight for the woods, running,
Jogging, stumbling, put a mile between us
And where so many comfortable years we lived.
To have read decades about the battle
Coming between Good and Evil, then to be reduced
To scampering in nightclothes for primitive safety,
Does little to help one put up with it.
All around is demon and angel, otherworldly force,
And the mind of man is best put to use
In getting Himself off the field. I pull my shorts
Tight to the waist, inspect bare feet
For protruding stubble, cuts. The angel on our roof
Swings his sword and our house by the power
Radiated in the arc is smashed. We collect
The neighbors' children, one burned,
One maimed by debris, turn up the first road

We come across. Far ahead
There is a crash and three young girls
Are made to jelly. We'd like to somehow
Walk out of it, watch the conclusion
From tree stumps on a hillside. The fire now around us
Like wheat, we can't tell angel from demon,
The work of God from the work of Beelzebub –
The flame is the flame, and a poor man's physics.
I take as many children into my arms as will fit
And shout *God be praised! God be praised!*
And the wife, her fingers already ash,
Strikes me for every selfish, spiritless syllable.

THE HATEMONGER

He comes down the road bearing a briefcase.
It is a hundred and one in the shade
And he does not sweat. The impression
That he has left his car parked under
Trees in a prettier part of town travels with him.
He stops to watch children playing
In front yards made of packed earth,
Shearings of concrete and waste wood. He waves
At a woman in her side yard hanging clothes.
His tie is pulled down just enough
To suggest a practical respect. The suit coat
Is draped atop the briefcase. He crosses the street
To speak in short sentences with a man
Rattling the bones of a car soon to be junked.
Dogs look up as he passes, make ready
To defend their territory, but would not think
To run to the edge of the road, bark
For him to recognize the full length of their domain.
Girls edging the street fall back to positions
Behind a fence as he draws near. Housewives
Watch from smeared front windows.
Men slap at mosquitoes more quietly than ever
So as not to attract attention. At the last
Ramshackle home, a house built for sharecroppers,
He ascends the steps in shoes that seem
To have escaped all of the ever-present dust,
Puts out a fist and knocks.
He smiles, offers his hand to the one who answers,
Asks to be let in, follows a startled occupant.

The pleasantness of his voice floats through the street
Like the sound of women dressed for the monthly dance.
The select house is the only one along the row
With backed curtains. Into the couch
The man sinks, leans forward to the briefcase
Left on a box table, sighs with opening it.
The head of the household with excitement
Rattles against his pants, peers over the lip of the case,
Turns to tell those gathered behind what it is like.

BALANCE

Fall. Gray fields wait like fertile women,
Their soils turned into other people's houses.
From the hill, the clatter-board shack,
A man, three women take up manifestations of iron
And run like children shocked by first snow
Into the birthing land. Frenzies of arm,
Wrist and thigh, the back and delicate waist.
Wheat, corn, potato, peeling flesh, sweat,
Gather circuses of dust and sun. Wind
Seductively tears the beauty from female form. The man
Is raising like the earth's icon his hand
While the women lift flax skirts to their knees,
Waddling to sit for lunch with warm tea
Beneath the oak spared its hillock in flat field.
Weapons are preparing for harvest; leaves rattle
As though the shuffling feet of some lost,
Once cannibal species. Even so,
It is raining next spring's rain
On the grateful, upturned face of a man
Making his prayer over animal flesh.

EVIDENCE

1. I shoot another snake.
The last one was a diamond back;
This one I think only a corn snake.
In some parts of the world
There are salamanders that look very much
Like snakes, but I think not in this part.
Were there any, I'd shoot them too.
The bodies are strung out for half a mile.
I am becoming a very good shot.

2. I can't remember whether
I get paid by the snake or the hour.
In either case, the wife is at home
Cooking beef, or cleaning the bathroom,
With our son making dust in the backyard.
The boy, no slackling, will have
Hard matter for his hands, in his head
The mathematics to deal with it.
No snakes are in the yard.

3. The rocks get warm and I sit in the open
Shouting out arguments of Veblen
The poetry of Rilke, lines of Hemmingway,
And humming Bach. All I need
Is for a head to peer around a stone,
A sidewinder to rattle a pebble,
The prey of a snake to dash for freedom.
I remember I get paid by the hour
And get two with one slug.

<>

4. The wife is pregnant; she spends
Her day waddling from room to room,
Clings to the stoop rail for strength,
And I am somehow proud of myself.
We spend our evenings at the table,
Reading books, discussing literature, teach
Our son practical motors, pulleys, calculus.
Outside, the wind is a banging against boards.
I've nailed the snakes to the side of the house.

5. One day you want me to stay home,
One day stay in with you.
You stand at the doorway,
The sun like sheet glass,
As I walk with the rifle,
Ammunition in a sack.
All night I've dreamed of snakes,
Of their fluid motion, their damnation,
My gathering the hot shells in a pile.

6. I sit on a rock.
All across the plain are tracks
Ending in scatters of sand
The deaths I've caused have made.
The snakes are beginning to crawl
In the same worn tracks. I hold the rifle
Still, pointing at the head of a channel
And while I'm away with work
You bring into our house a daughter.

MORALITY

The precision of things gets to you.
The leaf on the porch. The rake
Leaning against the steps. Your dog
Barking at cans tied to a post.
Along your arm your knife drags
And cuts the hair or does not cut it
And it is the same. The hides
Of three ferrets killed yesterday dry
Stretched across the fence and it would be
No different were a man's skin there.
The exactness, the sudden stops and starts,
The numerical perfection of everything
Gets to you. Along the lane
A boy comes to deliver a week's order
Of groceries and his skin pouts of sweat.
There is room beside the animal hides
And you think
At a distance
Aesthetics
Could be all there is in a man.
The act is strung like a door,
The elements have come to alignment just so.

THE MISTRESS OF DRAGONS,
AND THE MAN WHO COULD NOT SLEEP

You watch her step out, the sound of her
Nothing at all. She thinks you are asleep
And out of love she does not want to wake you.
She'll let her hair down in the hall,
Brush on, in the downstairs bathroom, a little
Eye make-up, dab the most available lipstick.
But at the end of it she is hardly made-up at all –
No more than for a trip to the grocery store.
She even wears flat shoes and loose jeans.
Once she's out of the house, you get up,
Move through dark rooms to a window at the end of the hall,
Leave all the lights off, barely part the curtains.
The beast is not much more than eight feet long,
His flame enough to start brush fires
But not to blacken buildings in one blare.
Undressing, your wife in the short grass and dew
Is the most beautiful thing you have ever seen,
Better than the land at sunrise, or the clover
In your yard before cutting. She climbs atop the beast
With the same movement she uses to put children to bed.
It would be the perfect time to kill the evil,
Your wife dragging him through sex
Like the pulling from water of a drowning man.
Someone could wait by the shed, slip up
And find a good spot between scales.
But this monster is little more
Than what a few men, a bit drunk
And with shotguns, could end

In one evening's stumbling, and you wonder
Why the woman puts up with it,
What she is protecting. Next night
The thing is thirty feet long,
A tail that could sweep outbuildings aside.
If ever they find out at the Ford plant
There'll be no end to it. A man should make
His stands in his own behalf, call out the county
If the nemesis gets too large.
Every night she creeps in, returning with the silence
Of aging, the commonness of cold in December.
The covers hardly moving at all she is again
In her worn spot, asleep almost
The moment the bed and gravity have her.
How well and quickly she sleeps.
For years you've thought it exhaustion, relief
That one night's horrible work is done.
Now you worry she has a life of her own.

THE NATURE OF CHANGE

We are a country that doesn't take to much.
The family is still the circle of activity.
Our Sundays are quiet. Patriotic holidays
The stores are closed. There is a little
Illicit whiskey, one racy girl in town,
But we keep as few words said as can, believe
In the overall goodness of things. So when,
Out of the North, this last fad started
We refused to let it in, let it take hold.
We've been through hula hoops, alligator shoes,
Marijuana, clackers, designer jeans
And God knows what else. It still takes
Each year for life good weather for planting
And harvest, adequate rain; you can still have sons
When the wife is unhappy about it. Yet,
The McClellan boys were all up to try it,
And not a few others had their sights
Set to it – so we nailed one dog in a box,
Put it to fire in Webber's field.
The kids seemed to enjoy it a hell of a lot.
I thought the mess to clean up – and we made
Them clean it up themselves – would have been enough
To put them off – but no, and immediately
They wanted to find another dog, or cat, and go at it again.
Change is not too well received around here.
But we put our children above everything,
And I do have a fresh litter of puppies.
Could be we'll mature with the times.

THE POEM ALMOST ABOUT BASEBALL

It's not your yellow fingers,
Clenched and hidden behind your back.
It's not your forward lean, the hat brim
Jutting out like a cliff over plotless ocean. It's not
The pin stripes, nor the chewing gum.
Nor the shoes dug in, one just barely
Touching the rubber. It is not the position
On the mound, the center of the camera,
The being slightly raised. It's not
Your shoulder, rounded like the end of a
Ball-peen hammer, wrestling under the cloth
Like animals over prey. It's not the arms,
Those magnificent strings, that union
Between the will and the act. It's not
Your squaring off toward the plate.

It is the throw. The pitch-out. The ball
In the air like a clutch of new mesons.
The son-of-a-bitch at first.
Safe.

THE RETIREMENT OF THE TATTOOED MAN

If you ask
He will point out the hearts that started it.
The first love, and then the one that had to be added
Because of the first. Then, his character in question,
A snake, a skull. When he has worked long
The dragon on his right arm breathes, riding
The skin as his fingers move. Generally
He wears a long-sleeved shirt,
Full pants. But deep enough in summer
You can see him stripped to the waist,
The sights of Marco Polo's expedition on his back,
Sea scenes at his waist, and on his chest
The symbols of masculinity that were
In the early years his pride. Saturdays
You can sit with him at the gas station, have with him
The same conversation as with any man,
Get on to how poorly his small farm does,
Fit it into the general decline. Children sneak up,
Hide in the woods by his backyard plot
Days a good heat is forecast and hope that shirtless
He will give them the show. He gets as much produce
Out of the ground he's got as any man could,
Closes his opinions with an admission of ignorance,
Keeps his shirt on when he should. Years ago
He married the bearded lady, a woman
Who seems to put her clothes on the line
An hour before anyone is up. Now she
Is a freak.

THE PRIMITIVE

In private we speak the old tongue.
In such an out of the way community
We occasionally speak it on street corners,
At small parties. It is said that now and again
You can hear the postmaster speak it –
But he owns the store two miles back
From the main road, and it is good business.
Couples teach their children the old tongue
And the children laugh. Yes,
The words run into each other.
The syntax is unpredictable. And the sounds
Of people in love with their language is heard
Most often only across long slivers of dark,
From hundreds of yards away where a man and his wife
Are arguing in a kitchen lit to be a local sun.
We covet the way the old words fit in the mouth.
Our children speak in angles and cylinders,
The jaw, tongue and lips ordered unnaturally,
And our children are what they can say.
They joke of the old tongue. Though with their words
They can call down stars, with our words
We live through them. We breathe
Into the mouth of the ancient language and it fills
Even our children's lungs. Goddamn them.
These are the tongues of light and dark
And we murmur awhile of the dark.
How great the light for the tribe; for the member
How safe the dark.

WAR EFFORT

The natives are hanging out blood-colored flags.
An enemy corporal, caught in the whorehouse,
Has been castrated and the articles
Hung upon the second-story porch rail.
The girls call to us and show us black garters.
The baker comes to his shop door
With loaves in each hand, offering
Food for freedom. He smiles
Like a child. Women are washing
Their underthings in plain view.
We are welcomed. Young children
Toss flowers at our column, rice. There are
Stories of the enemy: the tortures, the rapes,
The murders. Men and women in good health
Claim beatings, attacks. It is
The same at each corner, in each
Town. A man who cooperated
With the occupiers is skinned
Alive and covered in salt. A woman
Raped by an enemy sergeant and now
Four months with child is beaten
To miscarriage, even though the violation
Occurred but three weeks ago.
Young girls with leather eyes tell
Whole companies of men where at night
They walk alone. The tailor offers
The finest silk shirts, raw whips,
Stretch socks, copper stockings.
A boy abused by the past commandant

Is given to our doctor for inspection
And the man takes this sensuous boy
As gift. People are pressing against one another
Merely to get a look at us, our
Bright uniforms, gray weapons, lithe foreheads.
The brothel has changed all but the sheets,
Moved out of the closets the helmets
Of last month's army. We are ready
To take our place, to do what
Is expected. In the business district
Our scaffold is built, the enemy's
Left useless on the church way. It is
Who is doing what is done. I have
A young girl by the waist and she will be
Either the first or the last. Always
She has been bending to this moment:
I am pleased to be
More handsome than the antagonists.

THE MILKING COW

The gray field leads to a gate.
At the gate are rumors of freedom.
On your shoulders early morning crouches like a yoke,
Demanding support, dependent upon your solidity.
At your ankles grass reeks of dew.
In the roughness of your flank
Ground moisture hides, prides familiarity.
The open gate edges insolence.
Servility is no terror when enforced.
Light presumes your form, grants shadow,
Admits the nature of your absence
In the gift of warmth at your skin.
You lift one leg, and another.
Reluctantly, the gate moves closer.
Wind holds your shape in the air
As though it were certainty. Rough wood,
The half-rusted metal hinges
Make a world ordered in the open and shut:
The dimness of the land beyond the fence
Becomes copse, meadow,
Healing wood, benign fern, tangible grasslands.

Dumb animal, you do not think these thoughts.

THE STATE

You get the windows. I'm driving
Nails through the door casing, pushing your prize
Antique chest against the porch door.
Our son is under his bed, reading
With his flashlight. Up the street
The crowd is arguing with a man
Who leans out of his second story window
And soon they'll be pulling up his garden.
Regardless the worth of the rhetoric
A truck has pulled up to the man's stoop
And quick-eyed youths are loading onto it
The man's patio furniture. Washerwomen
Armed with stones stand in the road,
Weigh angle and arc. Janitors
With mops and brooms have caught
A young housewife outdoors and I'm afraid
The political polemic has come down to tatters
Of the woman's clothing caught on our fence.
I understand it's all about education,
Summer camps, the Skinnerian way our children
Are raised. I heard one woman screaming
How many children will be square roots,
How many decimals, how many quadratics,
As she had a middle-class girl by the hair,
Dragging her through rosebush after rosebush.
I share their concern. Our son under his bed
Laughs every time a rock hits the house.
Several people in the block worry the problem, worry to lose
The individual opportunity to turn to different mineral.

62

Support for them is so high that no one has called
The police. Different circumstances and we might
Be out with the mass, promoting our own
Rational alternative. A group angrily tugging
Their children from school I hear
Broke into a television repair shop, beat the owner
Half to death, ran off with forty-two
Television sets. The shutters shut, I sit
In my own chair, hand dangerously close
To the French phone. Outside day laborers
Pull the brass numbers from our mailbox,
Yell that our house is better than any two
Owned by the workers they know, yell
That all they want is their children's future.
I sit quietly with all that I have,
Wait for them to get into the liquor store three blocks down,
Grow frenzied a little while more, then subside.

THIS HOPE

The girl with the yellow rose
Wanders first into town at the east end,
Moves around the bakery shop – steps in,
Stands with her flower to her nose by the new biscuits.
The baker keeps his eye on her, has never before seen her –
Thinks most likely she will not buy, or buy
Only some light pastry for herself, for herself alone.
Back in the street she is soon alongside
The Patterson place: the private residence
Settled between two shops, the house
With the magnificent swinging bench.
The girl with the yellow rose stares
At the ponderous wooden construction
Suspended by small silver chains from the porch ceiling;
And from the living room window the youngest Patterson,
A girl of ten or eleven, fixes the yellow rose,
The girl. By the time the girl
Comes into the bar, everyone knows
She has been to the baker's, the Patterson's,
George's Hardware, the boathouse, even the Post Office.
An out-of-towner, wordless. The men in the bar,
Inspecting the white sandals, the yellow dress, the long stemmed
Rose, can guess only what to do with a girl like this,
Nudge each other, begin to bet around tables
Who will be the first to openly speak of it to her. With evening
No one in the corporate limits had not heard of her. Most think
That by now she has come to the McClellan place,
Or gotten completely beyond, on to the next town.
Groups of adolescents, both male and female,

Rumble half-drunk about the whole of the county
To see if they can find the girl with her yellow rose
Hiding in some back-lot shed, behind a wood bin,
At river's edge in the reeds. Next morning
Mrs. Leland has jacked the price at her flower shop
Of yellow roses by thirty cents each. Half of us
Want to go straight to the Patterson place,
Force them to tell us which of their roses
Will bloom yellow, and rip those out.
The other half are simply waiting for the girl,
And soon any girl will do.
All winter the whole goddamned community
Will be growing yellow roses in closets, back rooms,
Sealed in private places and with artificial light.
The only way we'll ever put a stop to it
Is if the girl comes through again.
The great fire of '78, and yellow roses
Were the first things out of their homes ordinary people brought.

WEDNESDAY EVENING AND THE OLD LADY

Rain has started to wear down
The cheap tombstone my husband
Doesn't deserve.
Leaving an old woman to scratch her neck
Alone should be honored
Only by a gravel mound under the highway.
Giving in, though, to the sense of responsibility
Thirty years of marriage brings
I still go Thursdays to the yard
And throw a few flowers in his face.

The favor is unreturned.
My garden stays bare, bleak
As snow on a tiny river island.
My garden clothes dirty from scratching
Like a dog, in a dog stance, in the garden dust,
I walk near fifty yards
To pick a few ground clinging blooms,
Their reds and pinks smashed against my fingers,
For the old man's death delight.

I'm lucky enough, though,
To be able to swing in a huge arc
From the small plot where I steal flowers
To the yard, to my back door.
The shower, then, is only a few steps
And I sit on a stool, letting the water
Dribble over me for minutes.
<>

The rest of the afternoon
I spend looking out my window at the boy
Who will scrub an old lady's back
For only a quarter,
And who still thinks death is a semi-colon.

WILDERNESS

The days are quick,
Bringing slight warmth to the children.

At night,
The moon settles like a broken bottle
In the snow.
Our fire is little against it.

Not even the wolves fear us
And come to the house
Half-way to knocking.

All in the same bed,
We listen for wind in the trees
And hope to hear the brook run again.
We wait for wolf-smell
To settle in our mouths.

As the cold grows enough to numb
But not to kill,
I almost wish there were no kindling.

BECOMING A CITIZEN

He shaves the waist a little thinner
And a couple in a car slow down
To give him one of those completely-
Through-the-skull looks. Only yesterday
He received seven notes in the mail – four
Asking why, if he had to carve a girl,
He could not carve one with clothes,
And three praising the anatomy of his errorless wooden figure.
Living in one of the dark parts of the Bible Belt,
Art criticism seeks a practical public.
A gaggle of local teenagers come around every dusk,
Are looking for opportunity to deface the structure.
He leaves the light on at his front porch,
Steps out two or three times a night to check
On the girl, her dark polish in the blackness
Like small light from the floor of the ocean.
Originally a square block that had to be brought
From South Carolina in a flatbed, each day
He cuts a little more, worked
Until the woman shape was evident, the complaints
Began. Two death threats
By phone, one by letter. These are
Good, Christian people, who can put up with only
So much. Thinner and thinner he pares
The woman. A month or two
And you'll be able to see through her,
On a bright day catch her shadow as you would
The shadow of wind in a child's notebook pages.
Someone eventually will get in, throw paint

Or put it to kerosine and flame. His wife
Worries the man's love of that woman,
Ties her clothes as tight to her sixteen-inch waist
As she can. One day the sculpture will come down,
The neighbors forget. She thinks of having
To move soon back into his room, around the house
Is as quick as suspension physics, skips her dinner again.

DECIDING ON CHILDREN

The man demands his allotrope –
I could find comfort in one.
Years he howls his expendable children into me
And is content with no issue.
As comely and usual as a house cat
I remain quietly the catalyst of his orgasm,
Growing to sway with his frivolous notchings.

His climax is not enough.
His whore must transmute herself into mother,
Prepare her walls for his puerile implantation.
The genetic certainty sung in hymns of DNA/RNA
Collaborating in mathematical sadism
Comes in his tubes like war technologies,
Forcing itself through carnage like a rabid dog –

Unaware, behind the curtain of the window opening,
Armies prepare.

THE ART OF IMPORTANCE

The corn each day moves closer.
Months ago I sowed its field,
Putting it on the west side of the fence,
Laying in the best of the land –
And a week later it began to come up
On the east. By the time it had gotten
A foot high already it had
Moved in under the barn, pulled the straw
Out of its way, cracked the boards,
Turned the tractor into mere rot.
Every time I look at it from the back porch
It seems to be still; yet each morning
It is nearer. Row upon row, now
Five and six feet tall, the stalks have torn
Through the grass of the back yard.
I will not let the wife hang clothes
On her line for fear. Only yesterday
At the edge I found the scarecrow,
A tattered mess of sticks and cloth –
Mauled and thrown out. I have
Resolved to make an end of it, but
Every time I set my fires the rain
Begins. Soon the corn will be at the house.
At night I can hear the horror
Rise even from the furniture. These years
I have made the harvest as easy as I might
And hope but the same for myself –
But the land, the land!
Who shall tell it when it is morning,

When it is night? Who will take the spade
And say here something will grow?
Who will make known to the weeds what they are?

THE BELOVED

Pie tins at the tips of your fingers
Call for birds. Sweat
Falls from your face to be absorbed
By the print of your shirt. All must be still.
In the trees at the edge of the field
Crows, sparrows, jays, a blackbird
Gather like shooting gallery targets on invalid limbs.
The muscles along the backs of your hands
Dance slowly to rattle the pans. Wings
In awe rise. In the North field,
The South, the East, harvesters frantically
Pull crops from the earth, moderate arms beating the life
For substance. Here, in the garden,
You wish you had tied your hair in a knot.
The long strands flap across your shoulders, distraction.
Yet, as ever first, the crows come.
Toying with the pans, they pick and preen about your anatomy,
Marveling at perspiration, your uniform flesh.
The noise of harvest draws about you like a curtain;
Already the woodpecker has been summoned,
A sparrow has decided where on such a device
As you the heart must be hiding.

THE COMING OF THE AUTOMOBILE

Father sat at Gunter's store,
Cigar in hand,
Beer on a disemboweled night stand.
The pot-bellied stove inside by a rag-tag couch,
Turned full up to warm the store's porch,
Blew smoke like a drunk's handshake.
Under the counter
On the inside of the swinging door
A tattered picture from an only men's book
(The style with only a whisper of a hint)
Hung from three corners.
Checkers flourished.
The talk of little nothings
Rose to oratory,
Drifted like the steam of artillery.
When the women so casually strode up
And blustered themselves into the store
I held back
Leaning on an old, far off hitching rail,
Amazed at their open-eyes calm.
Father goaded me to come,
An easy hand wave and head nod,
But I held to my rail
Like a plow horse tied there,
My hands turning red against the wood,
My hair made iron against my forehead
And dropping water like a dish rag.
When Mother came back
She stopped to listen a moment,

Standing like a distant relative's beagle,
Head cocked
A livid half smile creasing her cheeks,
Back half bent
Like the plow horse hugging the rail.

Two years later
Only she would let me drive.

THE STREETLIGHT

It went up without warning.
One night I came to bed,
Closed the window and shade,
And still I could not keep out the light.
I glanced from my room but could not believe.
In the morning, in my housecoat,
I went out and it was there –
Dull then, but standing in the yard,
Thin obelisk. Its metal beat
Of early sun. Better than two stories
It hung over the front porch,
The chicken yard, the path
Between house and outhouse.
It is not mine to question
But the place is no better for it.
The road is two hundred yards away
And only myself, my husband,
Our two dogs and unnumbered cats
Stay here in the house.
Light in day and dark at night
Is the thing: a lamp or two
Early evening is enough proof of mastery.
Over the fields night after night this
New center gleams and the crop
In its lurid gray grows confused.
The insects and the bats have a gathering place
Less substantial than the old: more alluring.
Years I have stood in my bedroom,
Drying after the bath or changing

From warm clothes to cool, the window
Open, the outside universe invited to me.
Now I close the drape – I am
Cut off. Each thing in my house
Is object of the light. Poor husband,
How shall I be the stop of progress,
How shall I make of you but outline?

THE USELESS CRIME

The winter farm has less work.
Time can be spent catching up. Canned goods
Are counted so often that each time
Their number seems to grow. A starving child
Eight thousand miles east is the end
Of a novel bought at the dime store.
Summer clothes are patched. Many hours
Are put to wondering why the grackles do not go South.
Always there seems to be stale bread.
Outside work is roofs and fences and door
Hinges and window tracks. A little trip in November,
Not much, just a run to the mountains,
Or the shore – to the tourist spots when
Tourists are not in season. Christmas, New Year's,
And thoughts of the soil in February.
March will be the hatred of rain or the lack of rain,
Mud or dust or worry that the good weather will not hold out.
Ice on the steps. The face in the mirror,
With its name. The unchanging name.

THE WHEEL

I have one too many spokes.
When we go round it clatters
And I have begun to wait out
The rhythm of its sounding.
Wood against wood it passes
Time and makes most minutes a pattern.
It lulls. Anticipation of it
Comforts me. One day for the battering
It will fall out. I will have
Just enough spokes. We will be whole
Again, turn for turn unbroken,
Pleasantly full.
The noise of the world getting to where it must go.

THE SHOOTING RANCH

The bird this moment is left on the ground.
Another, twisted in a box until
Direction is a useless belief, is readied
To pitch in the air: numb object
Bowled into the man's sights – the target.
The man is the rifle's device.
He stands at a place appointed,
Legs spread for the machine's recoil,
Red hunting cap, green hunting vest
Fitted about him like a ceremony.
Images of flight, of movement
Across grain and meadow, branch to
Branch, over water, the bird
Beats at the air as though it were
A glove and the man
Held to the rifle follows the affair
Unconscious. Nothing seems to extract itself
From the close dizziness. The bird moves
Like a wooden block caught in a massive,
Angry wave. Against the blue diminutive trigger
Warm flesh draws, terminating the penultimate confusion
Of flight. The bird
This moment is left on the ground.
In short, dark grass many lie like
Torn paper, spilled popcorn after the circus has left town.
By car trunk they go to the dump.
But first there is another bird.

FANTASIES OF THE FARMER

My arms are tired of chasing you:
Come back to the house. I can't take
This gaming principle anymore. Half a mile
From the porch lamp I am coming across
Your skirt on a low branch. It is a wonder
The cloth not torn and the buttons undone,
I did not catch a glimpse of you pulling it off –
Draw close enough to reach out
And barely miss holding you. Your heels
Picked from just by the porch steps
I carry one to a hand; your stockings
Are draped one over each shoulder.
Somewhere in the woods you are a blouse,
Bra and panties passing as the barefoot wife
Of a simple farmer. We are the people
That fail to understand the picnickers' jokes;
We are the kind who can our own vegetables,
Eat nothing a good man could not pronounce.
I am the bear and you are the maiden.
My J. C. Penney shoes crash through lost limbs,
Kick toadstools a yard before me to where
I am a venging, lumbersome horror
Hounding you to ground. The dark,
The white of your outfit, the blood track from
Your injured feet and thighs. A week
It has been and if not soon
I will find you only broken bone,
Rotted cloth, a rough place
For my skin to be worn against.

DIVORCE

The kettle boils like kettles that have boiled,
Will boil as women tie knots in thread,
Place children between covers
And comb their knotted hair.

(Make ready an evening,
Applying warfare to trivial things,
Laundry and the like,
Wedding rings.)

Kettle boiling,
Children in bed,
The husband half asleep
Hand upon his crotch;
You, to recite,
Speaking with a madam's tongue,
Speaking as leaves might speak,
Fluttering windward.

The divorce is made
And the kettle boils
As kettles have boiled, will boil
As you move his hand
And stir him to wake.

THE ELEVATOR

If you wait long enough
It will go down.
The button is still lit.
Sand blows in through the open doors
And no one answers the emergency phone.
The sun barely touches the horizon
Of a wasteland that runs the distance of sight ahead.
Yet by the watch it is one o'clock.
Push the stop button in.
Pull the stop button out.
The alarm bell does not sound.
A half dozen office workers late for lunch
Wait on the first floor wondering why
Their elevator takes so long.
Some take the stairs.
While remaining mostly inside the elevator
You peer around the retracted barrier guards –
Finding more of the desert, and a patch of green
Spotted far to the right. Two repairmen
Run their palms along the elevator's cables,
Guess competitively on which floor the car is stuck.
Sand collects in the stainless steel corners.
For the wind that blows heat and idleness
In swirls through the elevator, you would
If you could close the doors. Downstairs
Those who have waited long are advising those who arrive
That something is broken, and the stairs are best.
In the cab you think more of that patch of green,
That is the likely place. Repairmen

Check relays, replace switches in full blocks.
You write on the back of an appointment card
If you fix the elevator, send it back.
With only one lift in the building
It won't stay busted for long.

THE SALESMAN AT THE TIME PORTAL

I've not been through.
Some people end up in the center
Of Midwestern towns, walking the street
Towards a gunfight with no one they know.
Others find themselves at the back
Of a dog sled, rush and terror covering them.
It depends on the time of day,
The day of week, how
The portal is transgressed, and the individual.
Not everyone comes back.
Maybe some like it better there.
One man went straight to the bed
Of one of the period's more energetic
And available ladies, and tried eventually
To bring her back: when he stepped through
All he had was bone and an outfit that
With a week of coaxing his wife might wear.
I still wouldn't go through myself.
As much of a home-body as I am I'd end up
A mouth in a lizard's nest.
But you go if you like, the cost is the same.
All I charge you for is parking.
And if you are not back in ten days,
The car is mine. It is a natural phenomenon,
So I'm not liable. I'm not even sure
It's real time travel. One day the opening in space
Showed up by the garden, and I knew
Fairly quick my planting season would be shot to hell.
I've got no control: you will be on your own.

One man claims he left perhaps
Twenty of his bastard children
Screaming in history. I nearly had his car:
He was on the tenth day. He paid in cash
And told me nothing of the women,
Or how in ten days he seduced so many.
Go through, if you've got curiosity and the courage,
Come back to tell us all how, by the short hairs,
You took the other side. Here,
I've got the parking business to run.
Except for that, maybe I'd go myself.

THE PASSING OF THE SPIRIT

Think for some time of that troll in the well.
An area ten feet around confines
Even someone very small. All he could ever see
Of day or night was a flat disk,
The sun only a few hours each year
Visible, and then so huge in his world
As to be the world. The fistful of stars he could see
Changing only with seasons. And always,
The bottom of the bucket, the chord
Of the crossbar. Most of the well dark
For three hundred sixty days a year, all of it dark
For three hundred forty – imagine how sallow
His skin became, how even the blessing of light
The few days it would come would be nothing
But burn and the will to crouch in the water.
The things he would bump into on the bottom!
The old bucket, a pair of grass-cutting shears,
The bodies of a cat and a bird or so,
Pennies and rakes, stones. The hatred.
The bucket ever coming down, splattering him
With the water he smells in his sleep.
His thoughts to ride the vessel up, to climb the rope –
But the knowledge that he would be cut off
Halfway, discovered…. The well owner
And his neighbors coming back with fire
And shovels and grouse guns. His hatred
Turning the backs of his eyes purple.
His will to rise, to one night slip
Over the edge, the rusted shears in a hand,

Work a way into the house and wake
Every one of the well-users an instant before
He creases them through with his jagged blade.
His two feet up the well he has managed to climb
His greatest accomplishment. All those years,
Ice on the water, the rank humidity
In hundred-degree weather, the fearful
And tempting bucket. How many seasons would you last?

WEATHER PATTERNS

She walks in and out of the room
Like a circus. All evening
I'll be finding strands of blonde hair,
Seeing them float across the living room
Every time you get up from the couch.
She keeps our boy as tense as quartz.
Watching them walk and eat and drive
I think we'd better be ready
To take her in as daughter-in-law.
We could do worse. Yet, the last time
The boy and I went bowling up in the mountains
I thought it would be nice were he
To bring her along – and he said no.
The thunder rolled for hours. In her presence
He makes only small noises, cracks and words
And pops. Her face for me is too
Made up. She'll turn many a man
To hardwood, have gas station attendants quicksilver.
The boy has missed our last two games.
I fling the bowl alone, rattle
Half the valley when it strikes the pins.
The heart of her lies in practical alliance,
In being the common, only better done.
I'll be bowling solitaire almost a decade, with the noise
Shaking trees and homes less than should be.
Then, one day years hence, he'll show up,
Looking bored and smooth as glass,
Take in a short game, and after that more often.
Soon once more our noise will be over the whole valley,

Our double peels sending children to hide under their beds.
His arms will quickly be stronger than they ever were.

When I ask about the wife he'll say *fine*,
And with both hands around the bowl sight down the lawn.

JOY

A woman dances in the center of the street
With a bear. The bear is quite graceful.
He tilts his head, looks into
The woman's eyes, holds out his paws
Just to meet her outstretched hands,
And skips. No bear suit
Could be so well made,
So it is a bear. The woman
Is no bad looker, either. No wispy
Balanchine starveling. She has
A full chest, a substantial yet firm waist,
Cruet round calves and, through the flair of her skirt,
Legs that can do work. Most likely
She has had children, a husband,
Has gotten up at five in the morning
To be sure the water is warm. She dances
In a lightness more out of mind than body,
Not half as innocent as the bear,
Who seems to never grow dizzy.
They pass in and out of streetlights,
Twirl through intersections. The crowd that gathers
Travels quietly along the sidewalks, thickening
Three or four deep – some having
Raced home to awaken children and bring them
Into the thin night, where children stand cold
In broadcloth pajamas, pressed into their parents'
Thighs and coming out of sleep into the wonderment
Of being awake so late. The bear
Dips his shoulders, and the woman swings into the lead –

And then again the bear steps forward,
And off they go at twice their earlier pace.
Will no one save this woman from this bear?
There is no hat to place money in, no stand set up.
In and out of the overhead lamps they spin
Until they are almost beyond all lamps,
And ahead is only the morning.
About her face the woman's hair flies,
And she laughs, digging the breath from her shoes.
No one in the crowd will forget all night
They have let a bear dance with a woman,
All night. And into day.
Their shame is the music,
The sweat in the bear's hurrying fur,
The legs of the tingling woman.

THE MARRIAGE

You've kept him more years under the table
Than I can remember; how often
My knees have rubbed against his face
As I have eaten half a cold breakfast
I couldn't put to paper. We bought
The huge red tablecloth, floor length
On three sides and almost on the fourth,
To hide him when I'm working at the sink
Or busying about by the pantry door.
Around the edge of the dining set
I've crushed potato chips, cola bottle caps,
His bread crumbs. When I've left for the day
He's had you on the kitchen table, the sofa,
In our bed, on the porch; I find
Drippings from the previous night's meal
Ground into my living room chair. How you've managed
To keep the house reasonably clean, wash the clothes,
Stop God-knows-whose child from straying
Out of our yard, I can't figure.
We sleep quietly, though twice a week
I have my way on your side of the mattress
And fare not too poorly. I can hear him then
Rubbing life back into legs folded too long.
How, in winter when we turn the heat
Down at night, does he warm himself?
Sallow skin and brittle bones, eyesight
Gone to the lack of vitamins – I keep handing him
Under the table half my vegetables. You cook me
Double portions and still I lose weight.
I think I can go on fooling you forever.

THE CHAUVINIST

We cannot be made of those substances.
She tries to pronounce the words, is beaten
Senseless by the syllables, is closer to religion
Than her grandmother could ever bring her.
Numbers she suspects of carrying daggers
Concealed. We tell her physics is the history
Of inventive men talking to God in His
Native language, and she says she does not believe
Any longer in transmission, is reverting
To the default belief that in the television box
Are the actual people and effects. She is worried
That evolution seems aimed always upward, notes
That a spontaneous, Fatherly creation asks less of Heaven.
Music has suddenly gotten so varied, so broad
She falls in and cries for well-known
Ponds and creeks, well-worn backwater tributaries of sound.
She hides her books underneath her bed,
Announces biology is a mess she will have
Nothing more to do with, that geology
Has destroyed her trust in the land. We catch her
Balancing in the backyard, feet wide apart,
Her whole person waiting. To accept
An expanding Universe she wants to know
What she has done to make the stars run away.
We explain what we can, go to parents' day,
Sit, our knees cramped against desktops, with
The products of private passions publicly displayed.
Six days out of ten it is an argument
To make her go. Eventually, the fundamentals are resolved,

The world is fixed. She begins to see the facts
As means to unknowable ends. Then the boys come,
And she begins to forget: my anger
Grows to the pressure at the center of a sun
And I as well forget. I tell the wife
The first boy who sits on my couch,
His arm on her shoulder, and says he is looking
For a wife who can cook, I'm throwing out –
Bouncing once off the porch and showing the gate.
We find her books this time on the top shelf
At the back of the pantry, and her lessons
I read out so loudly that nowhere in the house
Can she go and not hear. The girl, with her will
Or without, I'll make more than another man's woman,
More than something light her father can give away.

REVIVAL

We've been sitting here long enough.
Already the Easten girl has been out,
Noiselessly under the tent flaps, with two
Of the McClellan boys. Our son has slipped by
And is with two or three others throwing stones
At the moon in the Sound. Any Thursday night
A man would put a tie on is a bad Thursday night.
At least eighty-five in this tent, the entire congregation
The smell of sweat, and this is what half a day
You left off housework for. I've been watching
Some girl I've never noticed before fidget,
Twist her ankles, dip her shoulders.
Mischievous, I run the back of my hand
Along the side of your thigh, catch the attention
Of the families sitting on either side of us,
See the irritation rise in your eyes like water
In a jar dipped below surface. It's going to rain
And we'll be caught running to the car unprotected after this long
Winded purveyor of God's knowledge is finished.
All the way home I'll be talking of the way
This dress when wet shows cleavage clear through.
Veteran, you put our son to bed quickly. Filled
With new saintliness, new certainty
About all the cracks and loop-holes in faith,
You'll be slowly unwrapping from wet things at the mirror
When half dressed I come up behind you,
Hands loaded. Never mind
Waiting in this unnecessary heat and maudlin fusillade.
After all these years, we both need reasons.

NIGHT HUNT

Two boys call at the window.
I come to the ledge in my long-johns.
It is eleven pm, but the rabbits
Are out. Already the wife is making a fire.
The rabbits are out. Why. No one knows. Must
Be something odd. The weather, wolves,
New construction, a flood. They leave trails
A foot deep in snow. I shouldn't come.
How often do the rabbits come out like this?
It is eleven o'clock. They leave trails
A foot deep. Already the wife is making a fire.
A noise in the barn. Cold muzzles, static fur.
The dogs are slipping quietly into their collars.
I put on my boots as they wait
Like a posse on the steps.
Someone raises his voice.
He is making deputies.

FIDELITY

The truck is almost empty
And we are nowhere near
Where we want to go.
Mother's prize stereo, the old
GE model of the early 60s,
Is left in the middle of the road
Downwind from the TV set.
Speck after speck the matter
Leads back. First it was the small
Things: clothes, toys, knick-knacks,
Lamps and tables. Now we are
Almost to the last of the electronics.
The possessions trail out behind us
And I could walk all the way
To what was home. Next is the couch.
To unload it and leave it in the road
Is tragedy enough – but after it,
There is little else. The oldest boy
Has volunteered to stand in necessary place,
To keep the trail intact. At times
I wish we had had more children.
The many must force the few along.
When we arrive, there will be nothing;
Nothing, save perhaps myself – naked, a line
Of loose change, pants shirt socks
And shoes, lint, my wife
Holding place in the road way back.
I am turning to salt and that
Is sin enough.

SALVATION

So you've not woken up in the middle of the night
For some time. I've still got
The kitchen to clean; you need
Take a look at the barn door.
I can't help it if you lie on your back
And snore enough to bring the roof down.
You move the bed; I'll clean under it.
We have our sex in a hurry, but it suffices;
It is no great matter that when I come
From priding in the bathroom you've already gone,
Turned about in the covers and slack. In years
You've had no nightmares, haven't balled the sheets,
Had anything but the dark, dense sleep
I've grown comfortable with. After
Eight hours you're the first out of bed.
The porch is one of your better jobs,
The rails straighter than an in-town carpenter could do.
Your stomach is good and you leave the booze alone;
I've not worried of other women in fifteen years.
So you shoot another useless goshawk. I'll pick the feathers,
Clean the corpse, find a use in the meat
Though I be damned with it.
Here, you bastard, the shotgun.

MISCARRIAGE

The women at the back of the house
Count fingers and toes. Children
Run in and out, blurred by the haze
Of fathers smoking on the porch.
The oldest relative holds the newborn
Coiled in her lap and is
Uncomfortable. Standing, pointing
At his leviathan arms, the Father
Calls across the house, across
The fields; his wife
Locked in the barn, curled in the straw
Like a plow animal, waits the one moment
When his pride will reach absolution,
When the rage is grief and biology
Once more but simple mechanics –
When he will forget
And want her again.

THE VETERAN

He sits at the edge of the field,
Props against the fence to drain a can,
And looks through the rows for a place to put it.
I worry now the wisdom of giving him his own field.
For months we've thrown away neither tin
Nor aluminum. He's been down to the Sound,
Pulled out rusted and slime-covered beer cans,
Hauled them back in the wheelbarrow.
I plow around his little land. Most often
I see him working with his fingers, burying
The cans half-way in at the top of his rows.
He's got them tightly packed – and, though
Of course they're varied, he's got them
Selected well. Every time he turns on
The irrigation I think only a part
Of the crop will rust, the other be simply cleaned.
He tends each object individually, and I roll
Around him, working only in bushels and acres.
He does occasionally use a hoe, and that's
A better sign. He puts out another can
And though he's growing short of space, I'll not pass him
Another inch of soil. He's got them
Almost touching, and he'll be planting them soon
In the furrows, making his own weeds.
It's silly; it's gone on long enough and he pops
The top on another can, begins to drain it.
Maybe by harvest we'll have our son back.
Or we'll coax him into being the scarecrow in his own field,
Sell the whole damn lot for scrap.

THE NATURALIST

There are other infidelities:
The cost of the light,
The silence of the frightened birds,
The wolf asleep.
You and I are not the center of the universe,
Nor a broken gear, nor even a whole one.
The chickens require feeding.
The horse could use exercise.
I could go into town,
Purchase a new yellow dress,
Turn my fingers to diamond and barter
For a pound of pure, unaltered salt.
We are not the couple mother and father
Would have had us become. After
The years of growth and approaching,
Of storming towards goal, we
Are not the mere sum of process
But process itself. There are
Other infidelities: there are some things
In this house that will not burn.
You have a shirt whose buttons are too loose.
There is straw on the earth of the barn.
Out in the fields we are raising crops
In ordered lines and our bed
Is yet a mess. Husband,
The fence for all its painting
Is still but construction:
In and out demands perspective.
My skin is the natural object
You have come to desire through practice.
I shall not be taken again without a struggle.

THE CHILD IN THE WELL

All night I hear her crying,
Small sound in stagnant water,
Voice just enough to keep a man
With a conscience from sleep.
I keep thinking how, if we don't get her out,
The water will go bad, our only source
Will start to taste like rust, turn thick,
Poison us. I built the well's sides
High enough, put up a canopy, made
The whole damn thing look like garden construction.
Only the near neighbors suspect it actually works.
Neither the wife nor I heard the splash,
Know whose child it is. No one
Comes looking; there's nothing in the papers.
I figure she must have sat on the wall,
Leaned too far over, made a clean fall.
Only when the full place is still, the wind is down,
Do you hear her fragile, idiot's noise.
Late spring, the water as cold as Vermont ice,
I'll clear out the sour depth, rake up
Her bones in one complete set. I'm never
So goddamned lucky. The last one
Was forty or more shearings. Before that
It was calcium mud. A month now
This one has been a sound in the deep
And the wife chooses to ignore her.
I'll not be responsible as long as she denies these children –
But the nights I look down to those eyes,
Listen to the limbs beating easily against predatory wetness

And console the tiny disruption to silence,
Are no comfort to me and I'll not forever
Keep the little ones from climbing out,
Pulling from the woman our shared waters.

PLACE

You think to hide under the bed,
Make the covers and crawl in beneath,
Peer out where the spread meets the floor.
This is no horror show. All over the country
The dead have been popping up,
Little decay among the lot of them – all
In fact it seems in remarkably good health.
Tombstones knocked over, crypts left open,
And it will be a mess for the groundsmen tomorrow.
I can hear your teeth chattering all the way
In the living room. I've made my own coffee,
Started my own toast, and it is the only thing
In twenty years you've refused me. Across the way
I can see Ned Turner on his porch,
Talking out loud to two corpses – and though
He is standing a bit off, it doesn't seem
To bother him at all. I see
A small group of them out by our fence
Trying to get properly oriented and I guess
For the older ones the land's changed hands
So many times it's hard to know in just
Whose gulch they were first put down.
One walks up the road plain as water,
Swinging his arms and strutting like a full-fledged man
Out to marry a blushing farm girl.
In a week Gloria Mitchel will be shacked up with one.
The light on in the hall, I can see
Your eyes loaded with white and locked floor level.
The thing's already come about, and in a moment

I'll go out smoking a cigarette, flag down
The first one I see wandering in the front yard.
Decomposition and pointed fingernails, and I'd be willing
To pull up under the bed with you; but this
Is a change, that, if a man doesn't get a handle on it,
Will pass him by like evolution the slugs.
There's a body laughing out by the shed and to sit
Much longer in this house would leave a man
Not fit to be husband. I'll tell him
The one about the dirty rag doll.
You pop the seal on our best bourbon,
Get yourself a good glassful or two,
Start to think like a woman having a home to protect,
Slip into something a little more comfortable.

FREEDOM

On this corner the man with the stone in his shoe
Stood for years, twisted so the traffic
From two ways could see his face full. I doubt
All that time the man had the same stone,
Or even if some days he had a stone at all –
But he would stand, his weight on the free leg,
Pointing with one hand to the shoe holding the stone.
The story is
His people were always the kind to suffer.
I can imagine evenings he would take the stone out
And consider whether this stone or another
He might have in his dresser would be less pain, and over
Years becoming able to hold against his heel without feeling
A stone almost the size of a marble, given it was round.
Early anger towards him in his later years was apathy.
Everyone knew how easily he could be free,
Free with as little as slipping the shoe off and dropping
The stone out, or one morning not placing the stone in.
Nights I am sure he would run his thumb
Around the depression the stone had made in his skin
And wonder why the skin was no longer red, why the calluses
Soon seemed enough and his freedom was a small thing
Compared to a new refrigerator or the neighbor's love,
But mostly why there was no pain and why the traffic
Going by mattered.

WIVING

You toss three balls in the air,
I pull flowers from a hat, our son
Casts knives at a tree. In
Southern Virginia you'll never do much
With a fair unless you have dancing girls,
A little burlesque. You light torches
And pass them underneath your legs,
Over your shoulder backwards. The boy
Is blindfolded, strikes the tree dead center
And I have fifty-two cards in all, fifty-two,
And I can guess which one you'll want.
Danville, Clarksville, Blackwater, Creeds.
The two of us they owed almost
A thousand dollars when the gates closed;
The boy came seven months later. I wanted
To run off with the snake lady,
Start a school for carnival acts –
But you grew like a pursuing noise
And I stayed. When the child was born
And I saw it wasn't a girl,
Couldn't in years be turned into money,
I should have left you then, caught up
With some of the old hands, put together
A small roadshow. If we play
Another backyard party I'll give in,
Drown myself and the boy in one of these
Black creeks they call rivers down here,
Let you run off with one of those
Hicks turned rich by the land boom.

If the child didn't have my clumsiness I'd swear
He belonged to the boy who worked the concession stand.
You spin a sword on one finger,
Roll two daggers through arcs stupidly
Close to your wrist. I am going
To put the boy in a box, saw him in half,
And in their lawn chairs three generations
Of small-time farmers made big
By expanding population clap as you catch
One of the blades in your teeth. The hostess
Is having her maid set us a little dinner
By the porch door. Potatoes. Carrots. Peas.
Roast. Rolls. How to hell
I wish you could cook.

MIDLIFE CHILD

The rabbits scrape their fangs on the porch's wooden posts.
The children in one bed because of the cold
Giggle, twisting in the covers like beached whales.
Frozen in the trees, wind drips in at our chimney,
Spatters on the window sill. Charlie-Chaplin-like
You walk from the kitchen with two cups of hot chocolate.
You are saying something about how,
In the pantry, even the preserves have frozen;
How the potatoes with cold are crisp in their pyramid.
Your ears, red, stand up
Like an elf's arrow ears. The steaming chocolate
Rattles around in my toes, your cold body
Settles into its niche on the couch beside mine, conversation
Pulls at my breasts with both dry hands.
There is something you are saying about the oldest girl.
Prankster, I will keep everything you give tonight.

RAINMAKERS

We take in as many black boughs as we can,
Linger on the edges of our toes. Many of us
Would run merely for the act of running. The hands,
Seen reaching down to gather, are no one's hands.
What all of this is costing us before noon
We could talk of easily enough, could
Curse and kick with gravel along dry ground.
After noon, shadows beginning, the salt marsh dark
And the woods graying, even the loudest
Fold their arms, are satisfied to stand
Upright, if to the rear and silent.
Every so often someone looks to the sky,
Or rises to stare head on into dust clouds –
And dozens gaze with him, their hands
Hard at their sides like salt beef for winter.
We wait like stones coming into their season.
At last a man in the center of the field
Begins to unpack from a crate all manner
Of tubes and wheels, works at setting all
The pieces out, while a compatriot uncontrollably
Is talking to us of the presence of angels,
Of how we must believe with both the left hand
And the right. Stooped, knots in the thickening evening,
Only those at the front listen. Great bands
Of metal and chain and leather. By the time
The machine is together we are singing
One ragged hymn after another, first verse only,
The nervous energy to drive continents together –
And with the sound of the engine firing,
The first sweet blue pound of smoke,
We are cheering, spinning arm in arm.

<>

It takes our minds off our troubles.
If we end up dancing naked,
Setting the base for a later increase
In population, so be it. It is worth all.
We need this one night. Blackness into the machine
We feed by the armload, out comes blue;
The stars flicker in it as though to get away.
Rain, and pulleys and wires will come with it –
Men in barns with unfamiliar hammers and elements.
Continued drought, and more than one fist
Will be put to the eye of God. The man
Turning the crank on the machine is giving out
Of shoulder, and the singer is losing voice.
The night as dark as the inside of a pants pocket,
The men change places.

THE ADULTERER

The cars go by twice as many
As any other day. The morning
Was almost any other work morning.
A few people have off the complete day,
Most farms start a little earlier,
Work a little slower after ten o'clock.
The children don't go to school,
Are a nuisance the whole time, could be
Put to more chores were we inventive.
It is the weekend. The wife
Will kick the kids out, tell the oldest girl
Not to let them back into the house
For an hour, for that hour will be
A woman as well as a mother.
The cars go by. Things since two o'clock
Have moved at no pace at all, but
Suddenly we are in a hurry, getting dressed,
The two middle girls, turning teenagers on us
At the same time, arguing over a blouse –
The boy wanting to stay home, but
The whole of two other families planning
To meet us there, he will go. The oldest girl
Is made-up too heavily and I worry about
Our having her act watch dog for our
Weekly afternoon hour alone. I've got to zip
The wife's dress and find her other shoe. In and out
Of the car the six of us move like
Birds awkward with long feathers and
Only in a county as small as this can

A family go together to a place where music is played.
We lose track of the girls in ten minutes,
Find one of the two couples, sheared
As well of children, and I check
Each passing boy for a familiar smell,
My wife's perfume on a too-young girl's neck.
I can't dance worth a damn, but
Everybody's got a purpose. I drink
Three beers and with two of my wife's
Homely friends make up enough steps
To have it raining all over the mid-west
For weeks. We smoke in one corner of the place
Only and there's that bitch,
Her long arms like evening willow,
Popping quarters in the juke box.

GRACE AT MIDDLE AGE

When he brought in the truth the first day
I thought where in this cluttered house
Are we going to put it. A wife,
Three daughters and one son. Enough furniture,
The most hand-me-down, to sit half the relatives
At once, all sort of knickknack,
A bronze-ish plate on the wall, and he
Wanted a bit of space for the truth –
Somewhere a little room to leave it,
Polished and so clean you could see your face in it.
My son – at this age chasing the truth
A little better than chasing skirts – I let him bring it in.
He was damn proud of himself. Imagine
A ten-year-old boy with a fourteen-year-old girlfriend
Who is pregnant: without knowing exactly what he has done
He assumes he has done it, glows with the doing of it,
Does not consider that perhaps someone else actually
Did it, and does not know what it will cost him.
So, my son. We took in the truth.
He kept it cleaner than ever he kept himself.
All of us were surprised to become accustomed to it
Sitting there on one side of the coffee table,
Placed so that perched at one end of the couch
You had to draw your legs under you.
A few weeks came and went. I had figured
He would tire of it; but he puts these days
As much care into it as the first. His hands
Shaping it are the muscle and bone
A planter would be proud of. He's gone so far

As to mold it occasionally into a footstool,
Prop against it in watching television. Like any man
I'd consider the truth a practical given,
The puppy you bring home that as a dog
Can get damned inconvenient. But he sees it
As the common acts – the desire I have
For the McClellan girls, the blood
In the steer butchered, the godawful noise
Often his mother makes in the kitchen.
When sometimes I carry him out behind the house,
The switch and a righteous parent's anger,
He carries a piece of it with him,
Holds it bent over glowering in two fingers.
He strokes it gently, reassuringly.
He is going to hold it against me.

IRON LOOMS

At the top of the hill sheep graze,
Placed among the dark rocks as though
Intending to stay. A few meters away
The boy acting as shepherd is throwing all his weight
Against his sister's best friend – planning after this
To make the rounds, cover all bases, hit
Each of his sister's friends that can match specifications.
The sheep never wander away.
At the foot of the pasture, the family's
Eldest girl is making an evening meal – potatoes,
Carrots, mutton. Father out back is bracing
The side of the house, cursing that the last storm
The wall almost came down, that the children
Were sent to the other side of the house
While the parents moved furniture away from suspect planking,
Watched water seep in at straining joists,
Passed from idea to idea of what
On such short notice to do. Mothers have been
Almost all day, in their gray, heavy skirts,
At weaving: lined back-to-back, row
Parallel to row, in the largest of social structures.
Huge, rhinoceran legs pump the foot pedals
As years before the legs took to the lunging of
The shepherd boy, the interrupt of his finish.
The women work their iron looms with the clatter
Of metal to hinge, the shaving of pins, the horrid slap
Of flat to flat. More threads are burst
Than are woven. Children are arguing
When matrons come home over who this year

Will do the most of the shearing.
Father steps at the door into the last of the light;
And the shepherd boy feels as though with this one
Even the small of his back has been shot through.
Above, a man from the next county is stealing sheep.

COMMON DEPRESSION

I do not know what you want.
The breeze on the porch is all of my mother's
"Nice" spoken at a thousand occurrences.
The Bartok rises like curtains at a window,
Has no trouble with the screen, walks
Out of the living room on its own legs.
I do not know what you want.
The Dreiser you've been reading came from my
Side of the library and I can't help it
If the paperboy sees no use in anything
Beyond Marvel Comics. The beginning
Of evening lies in the grass like proud weeds.
So the neighbors drink beer loudly,
Listen to top forty, have never seen
And hate ballet simultaneously. What do you want?
By an educated man's definition of the human
Most of our fellows are subhuman. Things happen
More serendipitously in our house than in theirs.
Our noises have more timbre. We have
Arranged the whole of our time more economically.
You look so small. I can't help sharing with
All erect, two-legged, speaking beasts
A common set of species signals.
We have the same depression in our bed as almost every couple.
Come fill it with me, and I'll wash the dishes tonight.

OVERTAKEN

The mist from the upper ridge is coming into the house.
You cannot stop it. Under the door
It seeps in slow, deliberate droplets.
Outside, the early evening dark is the same as ever.
The mist is absorbed into your rugs;
Hardwood floors are made spotted by it.
The dogs in the valley have found a stray rabbit,
The McClellan girl is again parked with a boy from the football team
Beneath old man Hodges' trees.
You have the windows shut, the door locked;
But the mist has soaked the end table,
Made the lamp dangerous to use.
On the couch your daughter and her date
Slowly grow limp with the water
And you are stoking the fire to no use.
You do all that you can
But your thighs are damp and your husband
Taps explosively the thick of his calves.
All about the house the mist has gathered.
The dogs from the valley have quieted.
The McClellan girl has become suddenly useless
In the back of Billy Jones' car.
The husband, dancing lightly on his water-fat feet,
Smoothly enters your bed, demanding youth.
Veritably, your daughter is destined for moisture.

THE BODY

You put your hand over your chest
And see the gray plank fence by the house.
The damn thing has no use, but the wife
Wanted it and four weekends in a row
You put it up. Yes, it does nicely
Close off the house, culture a garden a bit.
And the paint job on the house, a week's work
In the middle of summer, sets the whole of it off,
Makes a pretty clutch a hundred yards from the road.
Built in the '30s, that house is hell to keep up.
Poor plumbing. A heating system added on
With many seasons' savings. Windows that stick.
Too many floor boards popping up. The wife
Cleaning and cleaning … but not complaining, the house
The same house of the early courtship,
The marriage consummation. The faith
To be wedded in a church and make a bed
Squeal and sag in the middle. Good, solid
Foundations. The house has come through
Three hurricanes, the marriage more. Faith
You haven't relied on to keep the guttering clear.
Every morning for years up at four a.m.
Drinking coffee alone in the kitchen – in season
Working the garden, sweeping the back porch,
Changing the oil on the tractor you don't really need
But are proud of – and the woman
When you get back in finishing your breakfast
Or already washing, or in bed and you know
It is a bad day. At the Ford Plant

By seven. Huge hands swinging parts into place,
Parts that for ten years you haven't looked at.
Steady. Too old for one war, too young
For another. Time in. Laid off
Almost never for all the time in.
Huge hands. Arms with muscle that doesn't
Show, that hauls and lifts and drags.
Feet firmly on the floor, always with shoes that fit.
A body with comfort about the middle
But not too much – a good frame,
Good parts. Serviceable. A son to pass
The outer man along to would have capped it –
But whose fault, yours or the woman's,
Though you have blamed each other, no one
Knows. Years of the flesh. Putting it
Through godawful weather, sudden shifts
Of ease and power, strength and the light touch.
All that, and the fence, the house, this tractor
Getting old and done better by half a dozen
Part-time farmers hereabouts, the job
Clockwork, the woman and you gone mechanical,
The blood pumping. The eyes opening at the hint of light.
The nose piqued at fresh soil. Arms never
Folded in front of you, but dangling, ready
For the next labor. Let it go.
It has done what it had to do.

ALSO BY KEN POYNER

The Book of Robot, speculative poetry

Victims of a Failed Civics, speculative poetry

Constant Animals, flash fiction

Avenging Cartography, flash fiction

The Revenge of the House Hurlers, flash fiction

Engaging Cattle, flash fiction

Stone the Monsters, or Dance, speculative poetry

Barking Moose Press

Available at bookstore and book sites everywhere, and
www.barkingmoosepress.com.

www.ingramcontent.com/pod-product-compliance
Lightning Source LLC
Chambersburg PA
CBHW070808280326
41934CB00012B/3113